50 Premium Steak Dinner Recipes

By: Kelly Johnson

Table of Contents

- Classic Ribeye Steak
- Filet Mignon with Garlic Herb Butter
- T-Bone Steak with Chimichurri Sauce
- Porterhouse Steak with Red Wine Reduction
- New York Strip Steak with Peppercorn Sauce
- Sirloin Steak with Blue Cheese Butter
- Flank Steak with Chimichurri
- Hanger Steak with Balsamic Glaze
- Skirt Steak Tacos with Cilantro Lime Sauce
- Grilled Steak with Herb Compound Butter
- Pan-Seared Steak with Mushroom Sauce
- Steak Diane
- Cajun-Spiced Grilled Steak
- Teriyaki Steak with Stir-Fried Vegetables
- Grilled Steak with Avocado Salsa
- Coffee-Rubbed Ribeye
- Garlic Butter Steak Bites
- Steak au Poivre (Peppercorn Steak)
- Korean BBQ Steak
- Grilled Steak Fajitas
- Steak and Eggs
- Chimichurri-Marinated Flank Steak
- Steak with Mustard Cream Sauce
- Steak with Béarnaise Sauce
- Steak with Garlic Parmesan Crust
- Carne Asada
- Steak with Gorgonzola Cream Sauce
- Grilled Steak with Lemon Herb Sauce
- Marinated Skirt Steak
- Grilled Steak with Salsa Verde
- Cajun Steak with Garlic Mashed Potatoes
- Steak with Red Wine Mushroom Sauce
- Grilled Flat Iron Steak
- Steak with Horseradish Cream Sauce
- Steak and Shrimp Surf and Turf

- Grilled Tri-Tip Steak
- Thai Beef Salad
- Grilled Steak with Roasted Garlic Butter
- Herb-Crusted Steak
- Steak with Chimichurri Butter
- Steak with Caper Anchovy Sauce
- Grilled Picanha (Top Sirloin Cap)
- Steak with Caramelized Onions and Mushrooms
- Steak with Spicy Peanut Sauce
- Mediterranean Grilled Steak
- Steak with Black Garlic Sauce
- Grilled Ribeye with Rosemary Garlic Butter
- Steak and Roasted Vegetables
- Beef Wellington
- Steak with Truffle Butter

Classic Ribeye Steak

Ingredients:

- 1 ribeye steak (about 1 inch thick)
- 1 tablespoon olive oil
- Salt and freshly ground black pepper to taste
- 2 cloves garlic, smashed
- 1 sprig fresh rosemary

Instructions:

1. Preheat a skillet over medium-high heat.
2. Rub the steak with olive oil and season generously with salt and pepper.
3. Add the steak to the skillet and sear for 4-5 minutes on each side for medium-rare.
4. Add garlic and rosemary to the pan for the last minute, basting the steak with the infused oil.
5. Let the steak rest for 5 minutes before slicing and serving.

Filet Mignon with Garlic Herb Butter

Ingredients:

- 2 filet mignon steaks
- Salt and freshly ground black pepper
- 1 tablespoon olive oil
- 2 tablespoons butter
- 2 cloves garlic, minced
- 1 teaspoon chopped fresh thyme
- 1 teaspoon chopped fresh rosemary

Instructions:

1. Preheat your oven to 400°F (200°C).
2. Season the steaks with salt and pepper. Heat olive oil in a skillet over high heat and sear the steaks for 2 minutes on each side.
3. Transfer the skillet to the oven and roast for 5-7 minutes for medium-rare.
4. In a small pan, melt the butter with garlic, thyme, and rosemary. Spoon the garlic herb butter over the steaks before serving.

T-Bone Steak with Chimichurri Sauce

Ingredients:

- 1 T-bone steak
- Salt and freshly ground black pepper
- 1/2 cup chopped fresh parsley
- 1/4 cup olive oil
- 2 tablespoons red wine vinegar
- 2 cloves garlic, minced
- 1/2 teaspoon crushed red pepper flakes
- Salt to taste

Instructions:

1. Season the steak with salt and pepper and grill over high heat for 4-5 minutes on each side for medium-rare.
2. In a bowl, combine parsley, olive oil, vinegar, garlic, red pepper flakes, and salt to make the chimichurri sauce.
3. Let the steak rest for 5 minutes, then slice and serve with the chimichurri sauce.

Porterhouse Steak with Red Wine Reduction

Ingredients:

- 1 porterhouse steak
- Salt and freshly ground black pepper
- 1 tablespoon olive oil
- 1 cup red wine
- 1/4 cup beef broth
- 2 tablespoons unsalted butter

Instructions:

1. Season the steak with salt and pepper. Heat olive oil in a skillet over high heat and sear the steak for 4-5 minutes on each side.
2. Remove the steak from the skillet and let it rest.
3. In the same skillet, add red wine and beef broth. Simmer and reduce by half, then whisk in butter to finish the sauce.
4. Slice the steak and serve with the red wine reduction.

New York Strip Steak with Peppercorn Sauce

Ingredients:

- 2 New York strip steaks
- Salt and freshly ground black pepper
- 1 tablespoon olive oil
- 1/4 cup brandy or cognac
- 1/2 cup heavy cream
- 1 tablespoon crushed black peppercorns

Instructions:

1. Season the steaks with salt and black pepper. Heat olive oil in a skillet and sear the steaks for 4-5 minutes on each side.
2. Remove the steaks and let them rest.
3. In the same skillet, add brandy and deglaze. Stir in heavy cream and crushed peppercorns, simmering until thickened.
4. Serve the steaks with the peppercorn sauce.

Sirloin Steak with Blue Cheese Butter

Ingredients:

- 2 sirloin steaks
- Salt and freshly ground black pepper
- 1 tablespoon olive oil
- 1/4 cup crumbled blue cheese
- 2 tablespoons butter
- 1 teaspoon chopped fresh chives

Instructions:

1. Season the steaks with salt and pepper. Heat olive oil in a skillet and sear the steaks for 4-5 minutes on each side.
2. Combine blue cheese, butter, and chives in a bowl.
3. Let the steaks rest, then top each with a dollop of blue cheese butter before serving.

Flank Steak with Chimichurri

Ingredients:

- 1 flank steak
- Salt and freshly ground black pepper
- 1/2 cup chopped fresh parsley
- 1/4 cup olive oil
- 2 tablespoons red wine vinegar
- 2 cloves garlic, minced
- 1/2 teaspoon crushed red pepper flakes
- Salt to taste

Instructions:

1. Season the steak with salt and pepper. Grill over high heat for 4-5 minutes on each side.
2. Combine parsley, olive oil, vinegar, garlic, red pepper flakes, and salt for the chimichurri sauce.
3. Let the steak rest, then slice and serve with chimichurri.

Hanger Steak with Balsamic Glaze

Ingredients:

- 1 hanger steak
- Salt and freshly ground black pepper
- 1 tablespoon olive oil
- 1/2 cup balsamic vinegar
- 2 tablespoons honey

Instructions:

1. Season the steak with salt and pepper. Heat olive oil in a skillet and sear the steak for 4-5 minutes on each side.
2. Remove the steak and let it rest.
3. In the same skillet, add balsamic vinegar and honey, simmering until thickened.
4. Serve the steak with the balsamic glaze.

Skirt Steak Tacos with Cilantro Lime Sauce

Ingredients:

- 1 skirt steak
- Salt and freshly ground black pepper
- 8 small tortillas
- 1/4 cup sour cream
- 2 tablespoons fresh lime juice
- 2 tablespoons chopped fresh cilantro

Instructions:

1. Season the steak with salt and pepper. Grill over high heat for 3-4 minutes on each side.
2. Mix sour cream, lime juice, and cilantro to make the sauce.
3. Slice the steak and assemble the tacos with the sauce.

Grilled Steak with Herb Compound Butter

Ingredients:

- 2 steaks (your choice)
- Salt and freshly ground black pepper
- 1/4 cup unsalted butter, softened
- 1 tablespoon chopped fresh herbs (parsley, thyme, or rosemary)
- 1 clove garlic, minced

Instructions:

1. Season the steaks with salt and pepper. Grill over high heat for 4-5 minutes on each side.
2. Combine butter, herbs, and garlic to make the compound butter.
3. Let the steaks rest, then top each with herb compound butter before serving.

Pan-Seared Steak with Mushroom Sauce

Ingredients:

- 2 steaks (ribeye or sirloin)
- Salt and freshly ground black pepper
- 2 tablespoons olive oil
- 1 cup sliced mushrooms
- 1/2 cup beef broth
- 1/4 cup heavy cream
- 1 tablespoon butter
- 2 cloves garlic, minced

Instructions:

1. Season the steaks with salt and pepper. Heat olive oil in a skillet and sear the steaks for 4-5 minutes on each side. Remove and let them rest.
2. In the same skillet, sauté mushrooms until browned. Add garlic and cook for 1 minute.
3. Pour in beef broth and simmer until reduced by half. Stir in heavy cream and butter.
4. Serve the steaks with the mushroom sauce.

Steak Diane

Ingredients:

- 2 filet mignon steaks
- Salt and freshly ground black pepper
- 1 tablespoon olive oil
- 2 tablespoons butter
- 2 tablespoons Dijon mustard
- 1/4 cup beef broth
- 2 tablespoons Worcestershire sauce
- 1/4 cup heavy cream
- 2 tablespoons chopped fresh parsley

Instructions:

1. Season the steaks with salt and pepper. Heat olive oil and butter in a skillet and cook the steaks for 4-5 minutes on each side. Remove and keep warm.
2. In the same skillet, stir in mustard, beef broth, Worcestershire sauce, and heavy cream. Simmer until thickened.
3. Serve the steaks with the sauce, garnished with parsley.

Cajun-Spiced Grilled Steak

Ingredients:

- 2 steaks (your choice)
- 1 tablespoon Cajun seasoning
- Salt to taste
- 1 tablespoon olive oil

Instructions:

1. Rub the steaks with Cajun seasoning and salt.
2. Preheat the grill to medium-high heat and brush with olive oil.
3. Grill the steaks for 4-5 minutes on each side for medium-rare.
4. Let the steaks rest before serving.

Teriyaki Steak with Stir-Fried Vegetables

Ingredients:

- 2 steaks (flank or sirloin)
- 1/4 cup teriyaki sauce
- 2 tablespoons soy sauce
- 1 tablespoon honey
- 2 cloves garlic, minced
- 1 tablespoon sesame oil
- Assorted stir-fried vegetables

Instructions:

1. Marinate the steaks in teriyaki sauce, soy sauce, honey, and garlic for at least 30 minutes.
2. Grill the steaks for 4-5 minutes on each side.
3. Stir-fry the vegetables in sesame oil until tender.
4. Serve the sliced steak with stir-fried vegetables.

Grilled Steak with Avocado Salsa

Ingredients:

- 2 steaks (ribeye or sirloin)
- Salt and freshly ground black pepper
- 1 tablespoon olive oil
- 1 avocado, diced
- 1/4 cup diced red onion
- 1 tablespoon lime juice
- 2 tablespoons chopped fresh cilantro

Instructions:

1. Season the steaks with salt and pepper. Brush with olive oil and grill for 4-5 minutes on each side.
2. Combine avocado, red onion, lime juice, and cilantro to make the salsa.
3. Serve the steaks topped with avocado salsa.

Coffee-Rubbed Ribeye

Ingredients:

- 2 ribeye steaks
- 2 tablespoons ground coffee
- 1 tablespoon brown sugar
- 1 teaspoon chili powder
- Salt and freshly ground black pepper

Instructions:

1. Mix ground coffee, brown sugar, chili powder, salt, and pepper. Rub the mixture onto the steaks.
2. Let the steaks sit for 30 minutes.
3. Grill the steaks over medium-high heat for 4-5 minutes on each side.
4. Let the steaks rest before serving.

Garlic Butter Steak Bites

Ingredients:

- 1 pound steak (sirloin or tenderloin), cut into bite-sized pieces
- Salt and freshly ground black pepper
- 2 tablespoons olive oil
- 3 tablespoons butter
- 4 cloves garlic, minced
- 1 tablespoon chopped fresh parsley

Instructions:

1. Season the steak bites with salt and pepper. Heat olive oil in a skillet and sear the steak bites for 2-3 minutes.
2. Add butter and garlic to the skillet and cook for another minute.
3. Sprinkle with parsley before serving.

Steak au Poivre (Peppercorn Steak)

Ingredients:

- 2 steaks (filet mignon or ribeye)
- Salt and freshly ground black pepper
- 2 tablespoons crushed black peppercorns
- 2 tablespoons olive oil
- 1/4 cup brandy or cognac
- 1/2 cup heavy cream

Instructions:

1. Season the steaks with salt and press crushed peppercorns onto both sides.
2. Heat olive oil in a skillet and sear the steaks for 4-5 minutes on each side.
3. Remove the steaks and add brandy to deglaze the skillet. Stir in heavy cream and simmer until thickened.
4. Serve the steaks with the sauce.

Korean BBQ Steak

Ingredients:

- 2 steaks (flank or ribeye)
- 1/4 cup soy sauce
- 2 tablespoons sesame oil
- 2 tablespoons brown sugar
- 2 cloves garlic, minced
- 1 teaspoon grated ginger
- 1 tablespoon gochujang (Korean chili paste)

Instructions:

1. Marinate the steaks in soy sauce, sesame oil, brown sugar, garlic, ginger, and gochujang for at least 1 hour.
2. Grill the steaks for 4-5 minutes on each side.
3. Slice the steaks and serve with rice and vegetables.

Grilled Steak Fajitas

Ingredients:

- 2 steaks (flank or skirt steak)
- 1 tablespoon olive oil
- 1 teaspoon cumin
- 1 teaspoon chili powder
- Salt and freshly ground black pepper
- 1 red onion, sliced
- 1 bell pepper, sliced
- 2 cloves garlic, minced
- 2 tablespoons lime juice
- Tortillas and toppings (sour cream, salsa, guacamole)

Instructions:

1. Season the steaks with olive oil, cumin, chili powder, salt, and pepper. Grill for 4-5 minutes per side for medium-rare.
2. Sauté the onion, bell pepper, and garlic in a skillet until softened.
3. Slice the steak and serve in tortillas with sautéed vegetables and your favorite toppings.

Steak and Eggs

Ingredients:

- 2 steaks (sirloin or ribeye)
- 2 eggs
- Salt and freshly ground black pepper
- 1 tablespoon butter
- 1 tablespoon olive oil

Instructions:

1. Season the steaks with salt and pepper. Cook the steaks in a skillet with olive oil for 4-5 minutes per side.
2. In another pan, cook eggs to your preferred style (fried, scrambled, or poached).
3. Serve the steaks with eggs on the side.

Chimichurri-Marinated Flank Steak

Ingredients:

- 1 flank steak
- 1/4 cup red wine vinegar
- 1/4 cup olive oil
- 2 tablespoons fresh parsley, chopped
- 2 tablespoons fresh cilantro, chopped
- 2 cloves garlic, minced
- 1 teaspoon red pepper flakes
- Salt and freshly ground black pepper

Instructions:

1. Mix red wine vinegar, olive oil, parsley, cilantro, garlic, red pepper flakes, salt, and pepper to make the chimichurri sauce.
2. Marinate the flank steak in half of the chimichurri sauce for at least 1 hour.
3. Grill the steak for 4-5 minutes per side, then slice and serve with the remaining chimichurri sauce.

Steak with Mustard Cream Sauce

Ingredients:

- 2 steaks (filet mignon or ribeye)
- Salt and freshly ground black pepper
- 1 tablespoon olive oil
- 1/4 cup Dijon mustard
- 1/4 cup heavy cream
- 1 tablespoon butter

Instructions:

1. Season the steaks with salt and pepper. Sear in a hot skillet with olive oil for 4-5 minutes per side.
2. Remove the steaks and stir Dijon mustard, heavy cream, and butter into the skillet. Simmer until thickened.
3. Pour the mustard cream sauce over the steaks before serving.

Steak with Béarnaise Sauce

Ingredients:

- 2 steaks (filet mignon or T-bone)
- Salt and freshly ground black pepper
- 2 tablespoons butter
- 1/4 cup white wine vinegar
- 1/4 cup white wine
- 2 tablespoons shallots, minced
- 2 egg yolks
- 1/2 cup unsalted butter, melted
- 1 tablespoon fresh tarragon, chopped

Instructions:

1. Season the steaks and cook them to your desired doneness in a skillet with butter.
2. In a small pan, reduce white wine vinegar, white wine, and shallots over medium heat until thickened. Let cool slightly.
3. Whisk egg yolks into the reduction, then gradually whisk in melted butter to form a thick sauce.
4. Stir in fresh tarragon and serve the sauce over the steaks.

Steak with Garlic Parmesan Crust

Ingredients:

- 2 steaks (ribeye or sirloin)
- Salt and freshly ground black pepper
- 1/4 cup grated Parmesan cheese
- 2 cloves garlic, minced
- 1 tablespoon olive oil
- 1 tablespoon butter

Instructions:

1. Preheat the oven to 400°F (200°C). Season the steaks with salt and pepper.
2. In a bowl, mix Parmesan, garlic, and olive oil. Coat the steaks with the mixture.
3. Heat butter in an oven-safe skillet and sear the steaks for 2-3 minutes per side.
4. Transfer the skillet to the oven and roast for 5-6 minutes for medium-rare. Serve immediately.

Carne Asada

Ingredients:

- 1 flank steak or skirt steak
- 1/4 cup olive oil
- 1/4 cup lime juice
- 2 tablespoons soy sauce
- 3 cloves garlic, minced
- 1 teaspoon cumin
- 1 teaspoon chili powder
- Salt and freshly ground black pepper

Instructions:

1. Mix olive oil, lime juice, soy sauce, garlic, cumin, chili powder, salt, and pepper to make the marinade.
2. Marinate the steak for at least 2 hours, preferably overnight.
3. Grill the steak for 4-5 minutes per side and serve with tortillas, salsa, and guacamole.

Steak with Gorgonzola Cream Sauce

Ingredients:

- 2 steaks (filet mignon or ribeye)
- Salt and freshly ground black pepper
- 1/4 cup heavy cream
- 1/4 cup crumbled Gorgonzola cheese
- 1 tablespoon butter

Instructions:

1. Season the steaks and cook them in a skillet with butter for 4-5 minutes per side.
2. Remove the steaks and add heavy cream and Gorgonzola cheese to the skillet. Stir until the sauce thickens.
3. Pour the Gorgonzola cream sauce over the steaks and serve.

Grilled Steak with Lemon Herb Sauce

Ingredients:

- 2 steaks (T-bone or sirloin)
- Salt and freshly ground black pepper
- 1/4 cup olive oil
- 1 tablespoon lemon juice
- 1 tablespoon fresh rosemary, chopped
- 1 tablespoon fresh thyme, chopped
- 2 cloves garlic, minced

Instructions:

1. Season the steaks with salt and pepper. Grill for 4-5 minutes per side.
2. In a small bowl, whisk together olive oil, lemon juice, rosemary, thyme, and garlic.
3. Drizzle the lemon herb sauce over the grilled steaks and serve.

Marinated Skirt Steak

Ingredients:

- 1 skirt steak
- 1/4 cup olive oil
- 1/4 cup soy sauce
- 2 tablespoons lime juice
- 3 cloves garlic, minced
- 1 tablespoon brown sugar
- Salt and freshly ground black pepper

Instructions:

1. Combine olive oil, soy sauce, lime juice, garlic, brown sugar, salt, and pepper to make the marinade.
2. Marinate the skirt steak for at least 2 hours.
3. Grill the steak for 3-4 minutes per side and slice against the grain before serving.

Grilled Steak with Salsa Verde

Ingredients:

- 2 steaks (flank or sirloin)
- Salt and freshly ground black pepper
- 1 cup fresh parsley, chopped
- 1/4 cup fresh cilantro, chopped
- 1 clove garlic, minced
- 2 tablespoons capers, rinsed and chopped
- 1 tablespoon red wine vinegar
- 1/4 cup olive oil
- 1/2 teaspoon red pepper flakes

Instructions:

1. Season the steaks with salt and pepper and grill for 4-5 minutes per side.
2. For the salsa verde, combine parsley, cilantro, garlic, capers, red wine vinegar, olive oil, and red pepper flakes in a bowl.
3. Serve the grilled steaks topped with salsa verde.

Cajun Steak with Garlic Mashed Potatoes

Ingredients:

- 2 steaks (ribeye or T-bone)
- Salt and freshly ground black pepper
- 1 tablespoon Cajun seasoning
- 2 cups mashed potatoes (prepared)
- 2 cloves garlic, minced
- 1 tablespoon butter
- 1 tablespoon olive oil

Instructions:

1. Season the steaks with salt, pepper, and Cajun seasoning. Grill for 4-5 minutes per side.
2. For the mashed potatoes, sauté garlic in butter, then mix with the prepared mashed potatoes.
3. Serve the steaks with a side of garlic mashed potatoes.

Steak with Red Wine Mushroom Sauce

Ingredients:

- 2 steaks (filet mignon or sirloin)
- Salt and freshly ground black pepper
- 1 tablespoon olive oil
- 1 cup mushrooms, sliced
- 1/2 cup red wine
- 1/4 cup beef broth
- 1 tablespoon butter

Instructions:

1. Season the steaks with salt and pepper and sear them in olive oil for 4-5 minutes per side.
2. In the same skillet, sauté mushrooms, then add red wine and beef broth, cooking until reduced by half.
3. Stir in butter and serve the mushroom sauce over the steaks.

Grilled Flat Iron Steak

Ingredients:

- 2 flat iron steaks
- Salt and freshly ground black pepper
- 1 tablespoon olive oil
- 1 tablespoon soy sauce
- 2 cloves garlic, minced
- 1 tablespoon Worcestershire sauce

Instructions:

1. Season the steaks with salt and pepper, then marinate in olive oil, soy sauce, garlic, and Worcestershire sauce for 1-2 hours.
2. Grill the steaks for 4-5 minutes per side, then serve.

Steak with Horseradish Cream Sauce

Ingredients:

- 2 steaks (ribeye or T-bone)
- Salt and freshly ground black pepper
- 1/4 cup sour cream
- 2 tablespoons prepared horseradish
- 1 tablespoon fresh chives, chopped
- 1 tablespoon lemon juice

Instructions:

1. Season the steaks with salt and pepper and grill for 4-5 minutes per side.
2. In a bowl, combine sour cream, horseradish, chives, and lemon juice to make the cream sauce.
3. Serve the steaks with a generous dollop of horseradish cream sauce.

Steak and Shrimp Surf and Turf

Ingredients:

- 2 steaks (filet mignon or ribeye)
- 4 shrimp, peeled and deveined
- Salt and freshly ground black pepper
- 1 tablespoon olive oil
- 2 cloves garlic, minced
- 1 tablespoon lemon juice
- 1 tablespoon butter

Instructions:

1. Season the steaks with salt and pepper and cook them in a skillet with olive oil for 4-5 minutes per side.
2. Sauté shrimp with garlic and butter in another pan until pink. Add lemon juice.
3. Serve the steaks with shrimp on top for a surf and turf meal.

Grilled Tri-Tip Steak

Ingredients:

- 2 tri-tip steaks
- Salt and freshly ground black pepper
- 1 tablespoon olive oil
- 1 tablespoon garlic powder
- 1 tablespoon onion powder
- 1 tablespoon smoked paprika

Instructions:

1. Rub the steaks with olive oil and season with salt, pepper, garlic powder, onion powder, and paprika.
2. Grill the steaks for 5-6 minutes per side, then slice and serve.

Thai Beef Salad

Ingredients:

- 2 steaks (flank or sirloin)
- Salt and freshly ground black pepper
- 1 cucumber, thinly sliced
- 1 cup cherry tomatoes, halved
- 1/4 cup fresh cilantro, chopped
- 1 tablespoon fish sauce
- 1 tablespoon lime juice
- 1 tablespoon sugar
- 1 tablespoon chili flakes
- 1/2 red onion, thinly sliced

Instructions:

1. Season the steaks with salt and pepper, then grill for 4-5 minutes per side.
2. For the salad, mix cucumber, tomatoes, cilantro, fish sauce, lime juice, sugar, chili flakes, and onion.
3. Slice the steak and serve over the Thai beef salad.

Grilled Steak with Roasted Garlic Butter

Ingredients:

- 2 steaks (filet mignon or ribeye)
- Salt and freshly ground black pepper
- 1/2 cup butter, softened
- 1 tablespoon roasted garlic, mashed
- 1 tablespoon fresh parsley, chopped

Instructions:

1. Season the steaks with salt and pepper, then grill for 4-5 minutes per side.
2. Mix softened butter, roasted garlic, and parsley together.
3. Serve the steaks with a dollop of roasted garlic butter on top.

Herb-Crusted Steak

Ingredients:

- 2 steaks (sirloin or ribeye)
- Salt and freshly ground black pepper
- 1 tablespoon olive oil
- 1 tablespoon fresh rosemary, chopped
- 1 tablespoon fresh thyme, chopped
- 2 cloves garlic, minced
- 1/4 cup breadcrumbs

Instructions:

1. Season the steaks with salt and pepper. Coat with olive oil and press the herbs, garlic, and breadcrumbs onto the surface.
2. Grill the steaks for 4-5 minutes per side, then serve.

Steak with Chimichurri Butter

Ingredients:

- 2 steaks (T-bone or ribeye)
- Salt and freshly ground black pepper
- 1/2 cup chimichurri sauce
- 1/4 cup unsalted butter, softened

Instructions:

1. Season the steaks with salt and pepper and grill for 4-5 minutes per side.
2. Mix chimichurri sauce with softened butter and serve on top of the grilled steaks.

Steak with Caper Anchovy Sauce

Ingredients:

- 2 steaks (sirloin or filet mignon)
- Salt and freshly ground black pepper
- 2 tablespoons capers, rinsed and chopped
- 2 anchovy fillets, minced
- 1/4 cup olive oil
- 1 tablespoon lemon juice

Instructions:

1. Season the steaks with salt and pepper and cook them to your preferred doneness in a skillet or on the grill.
2. In a bowl, mix capers, anchovies, olive oil, and lemon juice to create the sauce.
3. Serve the steaks with the caper-anchovy sauce drizzled on top.

Grilled Picanha (Top Sirloin Cap)

Ingredients:

- 2 picanha (top sirloin cap) steaks
- Salt and freshly ground black pepper
- 1 tablespoon olive oil
- 2 cloves garlic, minced
- 1 tablespoon fresh parsley, chopped

Instructions:

1. Preheat the grill to medium-high heat. Season the picanha steaks with salt and pepper.
2. Rub the steaks with olive oil and minced garlic.
3. Grill the steaks for 4-5 minutes per side for medium-rare, or longer for your preferred doneness.
4. Remove from the grill and let rest before serving, topped with fresh parsley.

Steak with Caramelized Onions and Mushrooms

Ingredients:

- 2 steaks (ribeye or filet mignon)
- Salt and freshly ground black pepper
- 1 tablespoon olive oil
- 1 medium onion, thinly sliced
- 1 cup mushrooms, sliced
- 1 tablespoon butter
- 1 tablespoon balsamic vinegar

Instructions:

1. Season the steaks with salt and pepper. Grill or sear in olive oil for 4-5 minutes per side.
2. In the same pan, melt butter and sauté onions until caramelized, about 10 minutes.
3. Add mushrooms and cook for 5 more minutes. Stir in balsamic vinegar.
4. Serve the steaks topped with the caramelized onion and mushroom mixture.

Steak with Spicy Peanut Sauce

Ingredients:

- 2 steaks (sirloin or flank)
- Salt and freshly ground black pepper
- 1/4 cup peanut butter
- 1 tablespoon soy sauce
- 1 tablespoon honey
- 1 teaspoon chili flakes
- 1 tablespoon lime juice
- 1 tablespoon sesame oil

Instructions:

1. Season the steaks with salt and pepper, then grill for 4-5 minutes per side.
2. In a small saucepan, combine peanut butter, soy sauce, honey, chili flakes, lime juice, and sesame oil. Heat until smooth.
3. Serve the grilled steaks with the spicy peanut sauce drizzled on top.

Mediterranean Grilled Steak

Ingredients:

- 2 steaks (New York strip or ribeye)
- Salt and freshly ground black pepper
- 2 tablespoons olive oil
- 1 tablespoon dried oregano
- 1 lemon, juiced
- 1/4 cup feta cheese, crumbled
- 1 tablespoon fresh parsley, chopped

Instructions:

1. Preheat the grill to medium-high heat. Season the steaks with salt, pepper, olive oil, and oregano.
2. Grill the steaks for 4-5 minutes per side, or until your preferred doneness.
3. Remove from the grill, squeeze lemon juice over the top, and sprinkle with crumbled feta and fresh parsley.

Steak with Black Garlic Sauce

Ingredients:

- 2 steaks (filet mignon or sirloin)
- Salt and freshly ground black pepper
- 2 tablespoons black garlic, mashed
- 2 tablespoons soy sauce
- 1 tablespoon honey
- 1 tablespoon rice vinegar

Instructions:

1. Season the steaks with salt and pepper. Grill for 4-5 minutes per side for medium-rare, or longer as desired.
2. In a small saucepan, combine black garlic, soy sauce, honey, and rice vinegar. Heat until smooth and warmed through.
3. Serve the steaks with the black garlic sauce poured over the top.

Grilled Ribeye with Rosemary Garlic Butter

Ingredients:

- 2 ribeye steaks
- Salt and freshly ground black pepper
- 2 tablespoons olive oil
- 3 cloves garlic, minced
- 2 sprigs fresh rosemary, chopped
- 1/4 cup unsalted butter, softened

Instructions:

1. Preheat the grill to medium-high heat. Season the steaks with salt and pepper.
2. Grill the steaks for 4-5 minutes per side.
3. While the steaks cook, mix the butter with minced garlic and rosemary.
4. Serve the grilled steaks with a dollop of rosemary garlic butter.

Steak and Roasted Vegetables

Ingredients:

- 2 steaks (sirloin or ribeye)
- Salt and freshly ground black pepper
- 1 tablespoon olive oil
- 1 cup mixed vegetables (carrots, zucchini, bell peppers)
- 1 tablespoon fresh thyme

Instructions:

1. Preheat the oven to 400°F (200°C). Toss vegetables with olive oil, salt, pepper, and fresh thyme. Roast for 20 minutes.
2. Season the steaks with salt and pepper, and grill for 4-5 minutes per side.
3. Serve the steaks alongside the roasted vegetables.

Beef Wellington

Ingredients:

- 2 filet mignon steaks (center cut)
- Salt and freshly ground black pepper
- 1 tablespoon olive oil
- 1 tablespoon Dijon mustard
- 8 oz mushrooms, finely chopped
- 2 tablespoons butter
- 1 sheet puff pastry
- 1 egg, beaten

Instructions:

1. Preheat the oven to 400°F (200°C). Sear the steaks in olive oil for 2 minutes per side. Brush with Dijon mustard and set aside.
2. In a skillet, sauté mushrooms in butter until softened. Let cool.
3. Roll out puff pastry, place the steak in the center, and top with the mushroom mixture. Wrap the pastry around the steak and seal.
4. Brush with beaten egg and bake for 20-25 minutes, or until golden brown.

Steak with Truffle Butter

Ingredients:

- 2 steaks (filet mignon or ribeye)
- Salt and freshly ground black pepper
- 1/4 cup truffle butter (store-bought or homemade)
- 1 tablespoon olive oil

Instructions:

1. Preheat the grill to medium-high heat. Season the steaks with salt and pepper.
2. Grill the steaks for 4-5 minutes per side for medium-rare, or longer for your desired doneness.
3. Remove from the grill and top each steak with a spoonful of truffle butter before serving.

www.ingramcontent.com/pod-product-compliance
Lightning Source LLC
LaVergne TN
LVHW081501060526
838201LV00056BA/2869